King of Nothing

© 2023 by iAmBecomingPublishing L.L.C., Ashawn Johnson, . All rights reserved. Printed in the United States of America or Internationally. No part of this publication may be reproduced, distributed, or transmitted in any form or by any means, including photocopying, recording, or other recordings or electronic or mechanical methods, without the prior written consent or permission of the publisher, or visionary authors, except in case of brief quotations embodied in the critical reviews and specific non-commercial uses permitted by copyright law. These specific ISBNs have been filed with the Library of Congress for copywriting purposes of this publication.

ISBN# 979-8-9858540-7-7

I dedicate this to my children for being my positive output and highest achievement in my life; you're always with me I love you deeply.

"Read not with the flaws of the naked eye, but the flawlessness of the soul's potential sight"
- Ashawn Johnson

Index

Waking Up
Set You Free
Start the Healing
Sustain My Insomnia
Crazy
To Be Broken
Ghosts of What We Knew
I Feel the Love
Leaving L.A.
I Can't Follow
I'm Reminded
It
Temporary Illumination
Ice
Photograph
How We Started
Easy
Blood in the Water
King of Nothing
Shattered Moonlight
So Amazing
Forgiveness
Damage
Enlightenment or Insanity
Hello
Killing Me
Self-Inflicted
Hold On
Too Afraid
May My Pain
Please
Fix You
Die For You
A Daughters Love

Waking Up

Looking for a reason
Of hope to keep me pursuing
The reason for waking up...
I'm lost out here in a desert of the mind
That is filled with memories of you
How am I to exist?
If I can't feel your kiss
I will never again
I lost not just my lover
But my best friend...
Back to the heavens, you will go
And I am down here losing it all
Needing you to love me...
Love me once more!
The pain is taking all over
I can't eat or sleep...
The negativity is driving me
Pushing me into the darkness
Now that I've lost the light in me
How am I to get over it?
To believe...
Exist without my purpose...
Wanting to leave this place
Just to be next to you again
I'm stuck down here looking
For a reason...
Of love to keep me pursuing
The reason to wake up once more

Set You Free

It's fucking killing me...
Breaking me down to the core
To not feel your breath on my skin
See into your staring eyes
Laughing in slow motion
Thinking I've tamed the pain
When it's lying and waiting...
For passing memories to invade my mind
And drive me insane!
It hurts when I breathe.
When my heart moves
Of every beat of you...
That your name speaks spiritually
And I'm wondering, are you a mess without me?
When I know deep down you don't give a shit!
On to the next...
Bathing in his temporary lies and money
Empty comfort and dishonesty
But that's the type of woman you are
Running from the real...
That makes you question the false in self?
I held you up to the light!
As I fell into the darkness
And you abandon me...
Left me for the demons to feast
Upon my fragile mind and heart
With no mercy...
Just treated me unworthy.
And my love, just set you free...
As you have forsaken me!
To a lifetime of remembering what once was...

Start The Healing

All I see is darkness...
And I close my eyes and the pain drowns me
The hurt is so deep
From my mind, the thoughts keep rushing
I have no shelter
No peace...
My faith is in question
When love is all I've given
Humble and nurturing
Yet pain and hurt is all I keep enduring
I want it to end...
And I want the light to bleed in
I feel like my heart is dying...
My soul is fading
My knees are blending
For I have been praying...
But it's only getting darker
And my emotions are losing their feelings
In my ear are whispering demons
Repeating I'm failing
God! "When do I start the healing?"

Sustain My Insomnia

Bitterness consumed
Blood seeping...
Mental open wounds
You cut me to the core
No hesitation...
The damage to kill not my heart
But the soul so I wouldn't recover
I want to hate you so true
But I don't want to go to hell over you
Gave you all that I am
I would have died for you...
And it wouldn't have changed anything
You could care less
I'm so replaceable...
Because any man could do what I have
Another lie you'd have to live with
Ruined my life...
Just because you could
Too much of a coward to face your demons
Nightmares for your sleeping
Remembering the grass will never be greener
As my slumber...
Mind full of a mess
And I cannot ease the images
I can't forget...
Trying to sustain my insomnia
But love and hate won't let me sleep

Crazy

Trying to make sense of your actions
How you could disregard so much love
Pricelessness of purpose...
You have ill intentions only
So selfish to move alone
To leave me behind...
When I gave my soul
My very breath...
To keep that broken smile on your face
Hide so much from me
Of no empathy out of touch
No passion to hold me up to the light
Your intentions to cut me off
Into this free fall into the night...
As you took what little light you could
So crazy for me to believe
That you ever love me enough to save
To hold my hand and push through...
Yet you'd gravitate towards the negative
How am I to live?
Yet now I'm free from your poison ness ways
Toxic my heart is stained...
So it is best you broke away?
Or am I just a victim like a slave
With this broken mentality
Trying to make sense of the abuse
But I love you...
As you hated me
So how crazy do I sound?
How crazy are you to break my heart?
Knowing I'm all you'll ever need
And no one could replace that...
But soon as you rearranged
That mess in your brain!
You'll be the one that will look insane...
So damn crazy

To Be Broken

Unearthed too soon...
Needed more sunlight to bloom
To know thy self
To dig deeper into
Wasn't watered enough?
To have the strength to endure
The dry heat of life
And mistakes...
Fell to a false sense of security
Hoping true love would mirror me...
But lust is named and shame comes the same
Now my honest love is to blame?
Given all that I am
All that I have
Pulled through my hell to be strong enough
But get consumed by yours
You'd take no risk or have the courage to push
Just take all that's given and constantly use
I can see the light through my soul
Not so solid as it used to be...
The cracks are showing
A kaleidoscope of the sun and moon
Stars the glue...
Needing love to pursue
To be broken
Love Is a curse
That I've been blessed into

Ghost Of What We Knew

Everywhere I go...
I am reminded of your love
The beauty that you once withheld
Honest and pure...
I thanked God to be in your grace
To drink of your mental cup
So soft and true...
I don't know how I can make it without you?
The dream of who you were to carry on
I looked past the broken
The hidden...
For times like these to exist
Never thinking the bond would be broken
Never thinking you jump ship
When things got too deep...
But I will remember these things
That smile off your face
The long nights that held so much magic
The laughter so loud...
I touched you in a way no other could
Loved you in a way no man would understand
But you left me abandon
So here I am...
Walking alone...
Taking in the sweet heartache
Of the ghost that we knew
To constantly haunt me
Of all that we once were
To just shattered fading memories of you

I Feel The Love

You say you can't live without me?
I am all that's holding you together
Taught you that love is all that matters...
And slow and easy is the only way
As we vibe and connect so rare
You say and say, say and say...
But your actions reframe
Can't help but to feel the grass is greener?
Somewhere else you'd want to find out?
Because I make you feel these heavy things
Which release the demons in you
But the ones you like!
That keeps you in the night
Where you can hide and plot...
On how to self-sabotage all that loves you
Foolish things that your mind thinks
Ignoring all that is real...
Because of the lack of control, you fear
But you say that it's enough?
But sneak and lie...
Hurt me to make yourself feel ahead
As you think karma will never show
It hurt me so much to let go...
But the narcissistic ways you lead
Will leave you one day emotionally dead...
Amazing once our fantasy connection
When I felt the love...
Felt the lust!
And the darkness of you consumed our light
... of a false love that never existed in you

Leaving L.A.

No one will know our secrets...
The small and the hidden
Beautiful and amazing
The view of you... the travels
Embracing the heat and culture
Our connection...
Hardships and the danger you bring
Worth it so many times
Thought I'd lose my life to stay
Over my shoulder looking
Constant stress and worries...
The financial and cost of heart and soul
But you take it all
Without return...
Only benefiting yourself
L.A. will eat you alive!
Selfish and greedy
But the lifestyle is amazing
When it's good it's heaven
Temporary...
Of the next moment you could lose your life
Gambling to exist closer
Chance after chance she'd take it all
And send you on your way...
I've given my life
And you wouldn't agree...
Still hungry for more
A slave to be here...
And I no longer have it in me...
I'm sorry that you're not sorry!
But I'm leaving L.A.

I can't follow

I can't see the ocean...
Or feel the sand beneath my feet
No salt in the breeze my love...
I am lost and confused
Where have you gone?!
The heavy love has become lite
To the point that I cannot feel you internally
The glow of your eyes has dimmed
Such poetic words once
But now nothing leaves your lips...
You have traveled alone
Dark and down below...
To a place that you've sold your priceless soul
In a state of mind and heart unknown
To have a false sense of control
Cold the side of your bed I'm alone...
No comfort in your big empty
Selfishness has overtaken the beauty within
All so distant and full of bitterness
Heartless...
I've given my all of mind and soul
But you have become what I do not know
You've gone to a place my love
That I cannot follow

I'm Reminded

It's in the wind, ocean, and rain
That I could never escape the essence of you
The falsehood of the ending...
The secrets and white lies that broke all
You thinking you'd be ahead of the pain
The hurt that you caused us...
Deeper than trust
The blood that was bled
The hurt deep inside of yourself
That haunted you...
Those demons controlling your mind
Confusing your heart
Taking the sweet...
And leaving only the bitter parts
This is how you could walk away from me
Without a second thought...
Of the damage, you'd cause yourself
Because I can't be replaced
And no man would ever see you how I have
Or endure the pain you've insecurity caused
The games you've played and lies that were told
Maybe it was destined this way?
That like always I'd be left the martyr
To self-broken women
Who doesn't love themselves
Enough to love a good man...
So now our child will suffer
And you'll be too self-indulged to see
But I will remember the shattered memories
Because everywhere I go
I'm reminded of pieces of love
That was true...
But temporary in you

It

The soil is pure...
But the root is toxic
So frail the foundation built upon
These heavy dreams to sink into the sand
Never minding the view...
The corruption of you
Tainted intentions
The mission to bloom as other roses do
But show no thorns
Until all is comfortable and structurally sound
Your spot by the open window
Full of sun...
And love
But the Jekyll in you must come undone
Must destroy all so beautifully true
This hidden illusion of you...
It has its hands on you
Bathing you in insecurities and deceit
Biting the hand that soothes and feeds
With no regrets...
It will tell you to strike first!
It will tell you it's all about yourself!
It will deceive you to your lonely grave...
To reap what you have sewn...
Where all your demons patiently wait for you

Temporary Illumination

Amazing this connective flow of energies
Our hearts, souls are exchange in vibrancy
And we can the mortal existence expand
Ascend without action
But the natural movement of soul mates
Kindred and noble
The picture is clear
Heaven on earth
Every moment a masterpiece
Love at first inner sight
Yet as all things do in time
Diamonds and jewels...
Priceless pearls to lose their shine
And cost of value
Of spirit and of heart
To one day leave our bodies
Known that...
Everything will expire

Ice

I don't want to feel... anymore
Or think of what we were
One sided delusional frustrations
Heartsick that I am the one hurting
When every time you'll be ok...
I don't want to remember the temporary
The mental insanities of your immaturity
Dragging and pushing
The secrets and lies so easily for you spoken
Deceive me not... of your false love
You'd only be playing yourself...
Because I've done more than another would ever
Treating the priceless... replaceable
When the worth is more then you'll understand
Petty ness and a lack of empathy
And think you deserve good things?
When every time you destroy and ruin dreams
I want every care I've had
For you to leave my body!
Every ounce of warmth to part ways
And I will never again speak loves name
You were like the rest...
Weak, and mentally ill all the same
I will ignore your pain when you try to return
I won't save you if even you'd be drowning
Thinking the grass will be greener??
When you've been nothing less than heartless
I hope you get what karma you put out
And I pray that my heart remains
An icebox...

Photograph

I can see it clear
The difference in the wave coming
Into view the energy
In your smile and eyes
Temporary waters to guide your sanity
Thought my love once the remedy?
Once thought it was meant to be
But this is where the wave separates
I can see the perfection!
My heart is full…
In this moment…
But just a moment…
I love you!
And I know it means nothing to you
The grass is always greener to you
Until it's not!
Until the pain is too much
Until whatever game you thought would work
As you played it out…
But you will fail without me
Because my love was true!
And it should have meant something
But at this moment it's true
And I can see God in you!
And I know I will miss you
Crying tears of acid rain on my pillow
Knowing I'll always care more…
Wishing you would once just care
Let me photograph you in this light
Perfection is in this angle
How I will forever remember
Before the heartbreak sets in
And I will be the one…
The only one true to what once was

How We Started

Eyes burning of soul within
A connection so pure
A smile like that couldn't be faked
The rush of blood
Heart beating out of my chest
To touch you...
First sight "I love you"
Can't live without the vibe you given
Healing my broken heart
Clearing up my confused mind
The pain to vanish...
And the road so clear to the stars
Yet falseness has been injected
Killing the soul
Rotting the heart...
Zombie like eyes to peer into
Heartless actions and words
Now second nature...
You will reap what you've sewn
Alone...
Idle memories to be replayed
Such a fall from grace
Knowing this isn't how we started

Easy...

Bled for you countless times
Now there is no blood in my heart left
To feel more past the unclear and lies told
Gave you my soul so warm...
And in return actions still so cold
Immature selfish ways
Rather make love a slave
Then to be free...
Letting all these broken emotions
Only matter to me!
When the easy road is always just for you
So yet again I hold the burdens
Of all the wrongs you've done
Over and again!
And you still are too blind to see!
So you'd just push the blade in deeper
Blame and say harsh things
Because it's all you know...
All you will forever be
Tainting anything good in your life
Because you can't break the curse
Placed on the women in your family
But not my child...
The fire you'd still cause
Hurting everyone around you
Because your way is all you see
And this is why you'll always lose
Why you'll always be alone...
And why my love will haunt you
Because not once ever
Did you give me what I deserved
Or was easy on me...

Blood in the water

Purification of a deep-rooted bond
Beyond connective words but in silence
Do we find the core of what we truly are
Here I uncovered...
The hidden version of yourself
Among the ocean waters, we once floated
The lies you'd tell to cope...
To become someone else
Something of no spiritual wealth
Wash and repeat...
Your heart from light to darkness
This lost ark of self-worth in the mist
That I brought pure light
But it just reflected the light in the fog
The real me you'd be unable to see blinding
Stuck in your ways
Old waves...
That has to lead you back to the very dirty river
Where you had started
No growth or change to lift you back up
Like the evaporation of water
Back to the clouds to rain down this love
To free yourself...
Trapped in this endless cycle of pain
That you cause yourself and pass it on
This illness of hurt and anger...
Because deep down you don't feel worthy!
And love has made you question
It's very reality...
But false love gets your attention?
Back to a broken heart the mission
Because you'd ignore anything real existing
And lock yourself back in this prison
There's blood in the water
Of your interpretation of love
And you upset back I stopped drinking?

King Of Nothing

Powerless to the change
The position of the wind
But to lean against
The storm within...
Has torn me into pieces
Emotionally out of control
Consumed by the regrets of your actions
The failure of what in return I've not received
Captured the beautiful of you Queen
Placed her high above me!
She's been wounded...
Praying my love is enough for you
Yet you forsaken me?
Tear me into two!
For honestly loving you...
Try to distort the good in me
Unto what you've been used to
The light hurts your eyes
But your glow was so priceless...
You'll never see the worth I do in you
Rather cast your pearls among swine
Be wine and dined!
A price placed on you because of your beauty
You'd miss the purpose the reason
That together only can love rule...
Yet you throw down your crown
And here we are again
Dead stars that have burned out
Shining in a dark sky standstill
You'll search you in temporary others
When we had God in each other...
And I have to see your descent
Into immature selfish madness!
Falling for any false promise...
When you were my Goddess!
And now I am a man apart
A King of nothing...
Left in the dark

Forgiveness

Silly bitch...
I told you!
Now look at the pain you're in
Karma has found you?
I loved you!
Gave you all that I am!
A child, a family!
I gave my soul!
Silly bitch...
It was just too real for you?!
Tore down this beautiful dream
Thought the grass was greener?
They rode you wet and put you away dry
You confused lust with love!
Silly bitch...
I gave you my heart!
And you broke me apart repeatedly
I know you need me!
I know now you understand!
Now you're ready to be that Queen?
Now ready to listen?
To reason!
To be a faithful honest woman!
Silly bitch!
Come beg for forgiveness!
That you'll never receive from me again
Because I am no God...
And I do not have to forgive

Damage

Your smile gets to me...
More than I've ever let it be seen
I loved you I seconds
How could I resist?
An angle of your status
Beyond any dream...
Teeth in your smile
Fireworks applied
There's so much to say
Taking it all in...
Felt my feet left off the floor
Every time I'm around you
You do some type of magic
You could do damage!
Please don't take me for granted...
This kiss of your lips
Hearts beating as one
Away from you I'd come undone
I'd never forget this feeling...
No matter how dark it gets
Our love will burn brighter the most
As we get closer...
Please see I'm letting you in
I don't want to be hurt again
I don't feel the need to tell you that
Your eyes are so true...
I'm willing to do whatever it takes!
Allow whatever dreams to come true!
I'm captured in the sweet wonder of you
You could do damage!
Just promise to love me as I will you

Enlightenment or Insanity

The fear of falling is over
I've undecided jumped into a free fall
Staring deep into your eyes
Safety is felt...
My soul is damaged
My heart is broken
But I promise all that I am
Is for you...
Never felt this wave of emotions
Consuming over me and took me under
Into the sweet hold of you
I can see the stars in clear!
I can walk on water...
I'm so confused!
By enlightenment or insanity?
You've taken me to a level unknown
My eyes are renewed...
Amazing the surrender of free hearts will
Naturally how we just adjust and fly
A perfect fit you and I
Have I lost my mind?
Or found the true me in your eyes?
You rebirth me inside of yourself
Took my pain and showed me, love!
And now I know what a real woman consists of
And I promise in my every breath
To reflect nothing less than amazing things
That now again a dreamer can dream
A poet and again write of love...
And give to the woman he loves the most
All he is and she thinks it's more than enough
That is honest love

Hello

Hello...
I can't let go
Can you hear me?
Hello...
Of us do you still dream?
Or are you ok with how it is?
Hello...
Can you forget me?
All the love that was so true
Hello...
Have you given up on these things?
I've given you so many chances
Taken so many empty promises
So why am I the one again
To try?!
Hello!
Are you sorry for hurting me?
For walking out on me?
Hello!
Have you grown?
Are you now the woman that you needed to be
For self-love to be?
Hello!
Will you do whatever it takes?
Hello!
Have you given up on you and me?
Hello!
Are you done hurting yourself?
Or are you ok with how it is?
Hello...
Tell me to let go!
Or tell me to hold on!
You will fix things?
Hello!
Tell me you love me!
And you're nothing without me...
Hello...
Hello?...
Hello!

Killing me

There's a hole in my chest
Where my heart...
You used to be
Bittersweet this pain
To have had you at your best
And your ugliest...
The balance broken
And now you are memories left in the wind
Again... and again
Your insanities rain
Constant pain to endure
The lure...
Passionate love made
And honest times of happiness given
When you were lucid...
But there's demons at your reef
Once my love pushed against
Now you're looking for reasons to break through?
Sabotage our love once again...
All these diamonds and pearls
The world in our hands
Infinite joy in this place of ours
But this isn't the reality...
There's darkness in you!
That my love can't penetrate
So now you apart break...
You with a clear conscious
And mine full of hurt and pain
I can be replaced to you?
To me I willing to help you grow!
But the very thing I love
Is killing me the most!
You cut my hands...
So I had no choice but to let you go
But you will remember my warmth
In your world so cold

Self-Inflicted

Known in time...
That dark side of you would show
So I enjoyed with you the rain
Known soon you'd bring the pain
But I loved you... only
But the mental state of yourself was insane
Rather feel the hurt to cause yourself
When I was trying to hold you close
Place you back to the sea
Back to the stars...
But in return your insecurities
Would tear me apart
Thought my love would heal you
Could free you!?
And the moments we had
I saw that change...
Maybe it was temporary with you?
But I know you still feel
As I hurt the same...
So many times tried to love you so
But in return, you just let go
After I've given you so many chances to love
I'd heal and patch myself up
Just to let you do it again
Remove what I just fixed in myself...
Still, I don't want anyone else
Known you'll see it one day
But I can't just wait and stay
How I hurt me more than you ever could
In self-inflicted pain...
Just because of the rarities in our rain
I've endured it all...
For you to repay me with harsh and coldness
And leave me like it didn't matter at all
... again

Hold On

The struggle is deep...
In and every heartbeat I can feel
The distance between us being torn apart
Deeper it cuts...
Are you being removed from me?
But I can't get over it?
I don't want to forget you...
But I can't ignore the signs
For years I've been blind
Because I chose love...
And in return only pain I've endured
When I tried to hold on
And in my efforts gets me pushed away
When I desired nothing more
You are far from view...
So deep inside I am here again
To pursue all that I've lost beforehand
Feet in the sand trying to stand
A broken man...
It hurts so deep more than you'll ever know
I don't want to let go
But I can't hold on...
As it naturally moves me away and out
Back into the sea, I believe
The best parts of you are with me
And that's what gets me through
As it cuts so deep
I will heal as I can...
To be a stronger man!
To fill this loneliness
To seek a love unknown
When all my life I've been patient
So through hurt and pain
I'll allow it to be gracious
For I believe one day...Love will overcome

Too Afraid

I shake to your reach...
It's just too much damage underneath
To much unworthiness placed inside
Manipulated and shattered my shine
My focus is weary...
Fearing I couldn't see love clearly
I've been belittled...
Abandoned by the one who spoke of love
And took all I had within
Truly only lust then...
I felt my deep words aren't enough?
My pure attentions would just be tainted
Jaded and wounded...
I'm bleeding through the forest
After being shot by the heartless hunter
I don't know what you're after?
When only simple love I could give
I'd listen...
Give you hope...
And walk with you through the storm
Hold you close, give you passionate love
Lift you always up...
Be who I am when around others
As I would with you here...
Fight with you through the fears
Blend my soul with yours
To never be an end...
But it's not enough!
Never good enough to make her stay
She wants someone who has nothing to offer
And only false promise her...
The man she chases...
He puts his hands on her
Calls her down and out...
Pushes on her heart until she breaks
The man she wants the most...
I'm not that man!
I hear that you desire in my truths
But to be honest...
I'm just too afraid to love you

"May my pain and suffering, free you and give you peace!"
-   Ashawn Johnson

May My Pain

I hope you find all that you are!
And have prayed to be...
All that is meant to be...
The greener grass past our sea
And find diamonds in his lies underneath
I hope that he bleeds...
I pray that he gives you all you need!
Step on my neck until it breaks...
As long as you can now of false happiness reach
Then through down your gasoline
And set me a fire!
So no one will know that my sacrifice
Got you to this structured place...
Ignore the father I was...
How I taught them how to believe!
In themselves and understand what love means
How to follow their dreams
As you the same...
How I washed away that stain on your name
And taught you how to let go...
And believe in yourself...
How I forgave all you've done
And never left you...
You've broken the dream!
Torn apart all that I am at the seams...
So no stitching could ever fix me again...
Left to die!
While you're just getting by!
Smiling so peacefully!
And I'm dying!
I'm dying!
I'm dying!
But I'm happy that you could care less...
I pray for you...
May my pain and suffering free you
And give you peace
Because true love isn't just for yourself to see
It's for all that is a part of its dream

Please

The thoughts of suicide are heavy and thick
Like a mist...
That loving memories try to breakthrough
I am nothing without you
The peace of the better side of myself
It's missing and the darkness is coming
Calling my name at my weakest
I miss my babies
The pain is so deep...
I can't sleep haunted by loving faces
How do I pull through?
When I've always held the light for others
Made myself believe through all the hell...
But I'm too weak to stand...
A broken and weakened man...
Demons come calling quietly
Like whispers to pick up that blade...
To drive into the waters and just be consumed
By the very thing I've always fought against
I've held the light...
But now I am in shame...
And I feel I'm only to blame...
Where the hell do I go from here?
When I'm spiraling down...
Twisting and turning into nothingness
Where God's light can't penetrate...
Who would notice if I faded away?
Just another dead poet!
Then to become something more?
I miss my babies...
My smile...
Happiness that seems a lifetime away...
I'm crawling in the dark constantly...
Trying to make it back into heavenly view
With the easy way out so close to
That black exit sign...
I'm trying I promise!
It's so dark and I'm cold...
Please leave a light on...
Please don't leave me alone...

Fix You

I've lost myself...
Tying to heal you
I've lost myself
Trying to pull you into the rain
You'd rather remain dry
Deny...
That I am the one...
The reason for your breathing...
Your heart beating...
Of freedom!
One day you will see this...
This I promise!
I've hurt myself deeply
I cannot eat nor sleep...
But I know you're doing just fine
Being wined and dined
As I suffer in remembering...
It would be easy for you to let go
To break soulmates hold...
Because I am easily replaced?
So to you, I hope it last...
I hope that you'll be the woman
That with me you fought to control!
I pray with him you'll fully let go!
Because I never got that chance...
Just in the rain, I wanted to see you dance
Trying to fix your broken wings
And you just broke mine in return...

Die For You

I trusted you...
Took verbal hurtful bullets for you...
Been burned by the fire of lies
Dishonest family trying to hurt you
I stood right in front of it for you...
Laid my life at your feet consistently
But you stepped over me...
I removed the stars from the sky
And placed them in your dark...
Troubled mind...
So you'd be able in self to believe
That not everything is as bad as it seems
But still, you have no faith in me?
I've bled so many times...
Blocked out the truthful sun...
Of your issues, so you wouldn't be blind
And in return, you left me behind...
You slide this knife deep inside...
And twisted the blade to break off
To leave that hurt in me...
But what you didn't see...
That being one as we were connected
Is also killing you in these narcissistic deeds
Thinking selfishly...
That you're above and beyond all things
But you'll not be ready...
To live this now without me...
When once I'd die for you
I thought in living for myself...
Will define all that I've lost
Trying to love you...

A Daughters Love

How could you?
How dare you!
Step In between one of the deepest
Purest connections heaven sent...
Seeing how much she adores me
How much she needs her daddy's love
But you can't In yourself control
So you send the pain deep down below
Crushing her heart...
Poising her soul...
To grow up and be twisted
And bitter like you!
I'm a consistent father!
Held my little girl up to where she belongs
Yet you keep her around situations
That will do her damage...
Because you can't do what's right for you
So your daughter is supposed to suffer?
Because you don't want better!
And you get jealous of what we have together
How could you say you love your daughter?
But in the same breath try to break her father?
Knowing that I've been so good to her
And you can break take that away...
She remembers, she'll always know...
And the resentment she'll have
The pain she'll feel
Will be placed on you...
Ruining children!
Because you can't let go of your issues
Those demons that control you...
Idle minded thoughts and plans to hurt others
When you're only killing yourself!
You'd rather give her those problems
But say you love her?
When a daughter's love...
Should come before your own!
You're hurting her more than you see...
And I will be there waiting for her
With open hands...
When she's old enough to know
That you never love her
Like you said that you do...

www.ingramcontent.com/pod-product-compliance
Lightning Source LLC
Chambersburg PA
CBHW071231160426
43196CB00012B/2486